D1406744

A Robbie Reader

Class Trip
SAN ANTONIO

Karen Bush Gibson

Mitchell Lane
PUBLISHERS

P.O. Box 196
Hockessin, Delaware 19707
Visit us on the web: www.mitchelllane.com
Comments? email us: mitchelllane@mitchelllane.com

PUBLISHERS

Boston • New York
Philadelphia •**San Antonio** • San Diego
Washington, D.C.

Printing   1   2   3   4   5   6   7   8   9

Library of Congress
Cataloging-in-Publication Data

Gibson, Karen Bush.
  Class trip San Antonio / by Karen Bush Gibson.
     p. cm. — (A Robbie reader, class trip)
  Includes bibliographical references and index.
  ISBN 978-1-58415-811-0 (library bound)
  1. San Antonio (Tex.)—Juvenile literature. 2.
San Antonio (Tex.)—History—Juvenile literature.
I. Title.
  F394.S2114G53 2010
  976.4'351—dc22

                              2009001111

                                        PLB

CONTENTS

SAN ANTONIO

San Antonio's landmark Tower Life Building, completed in 1929, is reflected in a section of the San Antonio River. Right: Davy Crockett

A Texas Classroom

Maria hung her backpack on one of the hooks along the back wall of her classroom. She smiled at her friends, Maddie and Holly, before sitting down at her desk. The bell rang to announce the start of the school day.

"Everyone, please be seated," Ms. Hughes announced as she clapped her hands. The classroom grew quieter, and every eye was on the fourth-grade teacher. "I hope you won't be too disappointed, but I've postponed the spelling test until after lunch. Instead this morning, we'll be talking about a special place."

The students began murmuring to each other with excitement, wondering what the special place might be.

"First of all, let's talk a little about the state that we live in," Ms. Hughes said. "There are many interesting facts about Texas. Can anyone tell me one?"

Almost every hand in the classroom went up. Most of the students at Lincoln Elementary School had lived in Texas their entire lives. They started shouting out things they knew about their home state.

"It's the second largest state."

"People sometimes call it the Lone Star State."

"Texas borders Mexico."

"A lot of people who live in Texas speak Spanish."

The students continued shouting out Texas facts for a couple of minutes. When Ms. Hughes raised her hand, everyone grew quiet.

"Very good. I'm so glad you all know so much about our state," Ms. Hughes said. She walked to the chalkboard at the front of the room and pulled on a ring that brought a map down.

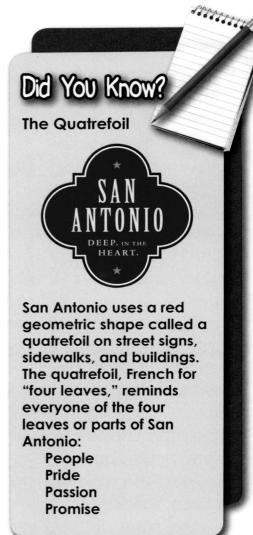

Did You Know?

The Quatrefoil

SAN ANTONIO

DEEP. IN THE HEART.

San Antonio uses a red geometric shape called a quatrefoil on street signs, sidewalks, and buildings. The quatrefoil, French for "four leaves," reminds everyone of the four leaves or parts of San Antonio:
    People
    Pride
    Passion
    Promise

"Now, can anyone show me where Texas is on this map of the United States?"

Maria raised her hand, hoping that Ms. Hughes could see it among all the other hands in the air. She was rewarded when she heard her name. She skipped to the front of the room and pointed to Texas, a large state in the center of the bottom of the map.

"Yes, that is Texas. We're in the southern part of the United States. Most people say that Texas is in the Southwest," the teacher answered. "Maria, could you stay by the map and find the cities in Texas that your classmates call out?"

Maria nodded, but was nervous that she wouldn't be able to find the cities. She didn't need to worry. When people called out cities like Dallas and Houston, she found them easily. She also found Amarillo, El Paso, and Austin, which was close to their hometown of Taylor.

"Can anyone tell me the name of another city that is a very important part of Texas history?" Ms. Hughes asked.

Classmates looked at each other, but no one answered. Maria looked back at the United States map and studied Texas. She looked along the Gulf of Mexico at the southeast side. She saw cities, lakes, and rivers. One river ran through a city they hadn't named yet.

San Antonio

Texas

Mission Trail
(Approximate)

San Antonio
Alamo

Mission
Concepción

Mission
San Francisco

Mission
San José

Mission
San Juan

Mission
Espada

1 San Antonio Museum of Art
2 SeaWorld
3 The Alamo
4 San Fernando Cathedral
5 San Antonio River Walk
 (Main Area—blue)
6 San Jacinto
7 Tower of the Americas
8 Institute of Texan Cultures
9 Market Square
10 Mission Concepción

"Ms. Hughes?" Maria asked. "Could it be San Antonio?"

"Yes, it is, Maria. Very good. You may return to your desk now," Ms. Hughes said.

Ms. Hughes pulled down another map. It was almost as large as the map of the United States,

A cowboy hat

but this one showed only Texas. Ms. Hughes pointed to a large dot near the bottom of the map.

"Here," she said, "is San Antonio. It is located in south-central Texas and is closer to the border with Mexico than to any of our neighboring states. Have any of you ever visited San Antonio?"

A few hands went up. Maria raised hers halfway. She knew she had visited cousins in San Antonio long ago, but she didn't remember anything about the city.

"I have a surprise for the class," Ms. Hughes announced. "We're all going to visit San Antonio very soon on a field trip. Before we go, we'll learn about San Antonio, the second largest city in Texas."

SAN ANTONIO

Mission Concepción is one of five missions located in San Antonio. Founded in 1755, it is the oldest unrestored church in America. Right: Father Antonio Olivares

Chapter 2

The Missions of San Antonio

Maria looked over the front seat of the car to see why they weren't moving. Many cars sat in front of them, but they weren't going anywhere.

"I'm going to be late for school," she mumbled.

"Something special happening today?" her dad asked from the driver's seat.

"We're going to talk about the Co . . . co . . . pecans."

"Copecans?"

"A group of Native Americans that settled in San Antonio a long time ago. They have a really long name," Maria explained.

"Do you think it might be the Coahuiltecans?" her dad asked. He pronounced it *kwah-WEEL-tih-kans.*

"That's it. Anyway," said Maria. "Ms. Hughes said the Coahuiltecans were a peaceful people who lived in southern Texas when the Spanish explorers came."

"I'll bet the Coahuiltecans never had to battle traffic like this," her dad answered.

"Of course not," said Maria. "They had to battle the Comanches!"

Traffic started moving again. Maria's dad dropped her off in front of the school, with plenty of time to get to her classroom. She was in her seat when the bell rang, just like everybody else in class.

"Good morning, class." Ms. Hughes smiled. "Are you ready to hear more about San Antonio?"

After everyone answered with an enthusiastic yes, the teacher began.

The area that would become San Antonio was a popular place for Native American tribes because of the winding San Antonio River. **Nomadic** tribes like the Comanche and Apache liked to stop and rest by the water before moving on. Other groups, like the Papaya and Coahuiltecans, preferred staying in one place and growing their own food.

These peaceful bands met the Spanish expeditions that explored the area in 1691 and 1709. In 1718, Father Antonio Olivares established a mission on the banks of the river. He named it San Antonio de Valero after the viceroy of New Spain. Soon afterward, a military fort called San Antonio de Béxar **Presidio** was founded, and the town grew from that.

In all, San Antonio has five missions. Mission San José y San Miguel de Aguayo was built two years after San Antonio de Valero. Three other missions to the northeast had trouble with **drought** and disease, so Missions Concepción, Espada, and San Juan relocated to San

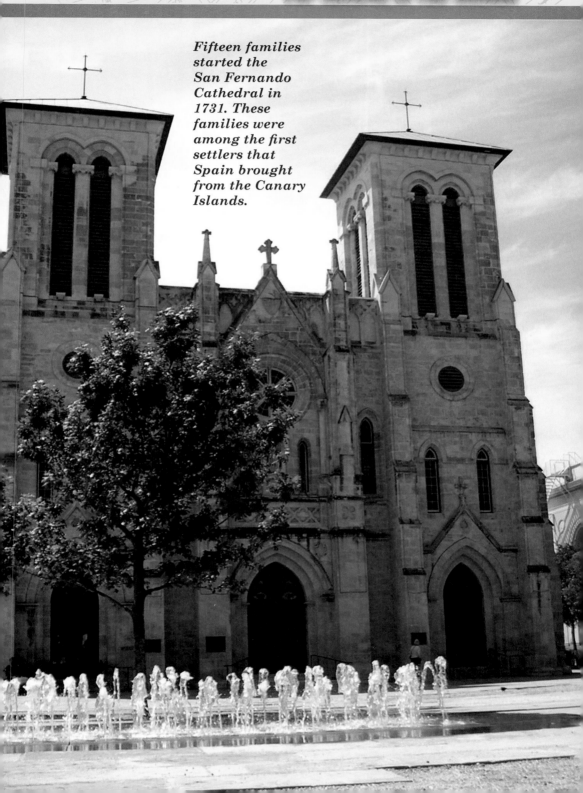

Fifteen families started the San Fernando Cathedral in 1731. These families were among the first settlers that Spain brought from the Canary Islands.

Antonio in 1731. The mission system flourished in the San Antonio valley for a number of years.

The Spanish missions weren't only churches, but also communities where missionaries and Native Americans lived and worked. Catholic missionaries taught Catholicism along with how to make soap and spin thread. The missionaries also put the native people to work digging ditches for an **aqueduct** (AK-wuh-dukt) system that would benefit farms. Perhaps most important to the Coahuiltecans was that the missions protected them from bands of their enemies.

The Spanish government sent a group of Spanish colonists from the Canary Islands to settle in San

Ranchers drove cattle to San Antonio in the late nineteenth century. The cowboy tradition has continued with the rodeo. In 2009, the San Antonio Stock Show and Rodeo celebrated its 60th year.

Antonio. When they arrived in March 1731, the settlers built homes and buildings around two **plazas**, Military Plaza and Main Plaza (later Alamo Plaza). Their settlement, which was part of San Antonio, was the villa of San Fernando de Béxar (pronounced "bear"). San Antonio became the seat of government for New Spain in 1772. Eventually, mission life declined. The first mission, Mission San Antonio de Valero, became a military fort in the 1800s. It is better known as the Alamo.

Did You Know?

The Alamo is more than a famous battle site. It also served as a mission, a military fort, a government storage facility, and a store. When it was scheduled to be torn down in 1905, the Daughters of the Republic of Texas rescued and restored the Alamo.

An American named Moses Austin was granted permission to bring about 300 American families to settle in San Antonio. By the time Mexico won its independence from Spain in 1821, San Antonio was filled with people from Spain, Mexico, and the United States. These **Texians** saw themselves as different from the rest of Mexico and wanted to form their own country, the Republic of Texas. The population included Tejanos (tay-HAH-nohs), people with a **Hispanic** or Latin background, and Texians, people who originally came from the United States.

In 1836, Texians gathered at the Alamo to battle Mexican soldiers under the command of Mexico's president, General Santa Anna. People like Jim Bowie and Davy Crockett joined the fight for Texas. While the Texians and Americans put up a good fight, they were hopelessly outnumbered. The battle after a twelve-day **siege** left most dead. Twelve people are believed to have survived, but this number cannot be confirmed.

Approximately six weeks later, General Sam Houston led Texians into battle against Santa Anna's armies at nearby San Jacinto, near the Texas coast. With Texians shouting, "Remember the Alamo!" they won the battle for independence, and the Republic of Texas was born. San Antonio became the seat of the new government.

Disease and Indian attacks led to the decline of San Antonio's population. By the time Texas became

Texians and Mexican soldiers battle at the Alamo. Many stories of the Alamo have reached the status of legend. Because so many died in the battle, it's hard to know what actually happened.

Texas Longhorn are a hardy breed of cattle that once thrived in the Southwest. They are often identified by the impressive span of their horns. The San Antonio Stock Show and Rodeo kicks off each year with a cattle drive through downtown San Antonio.

the twenty-eighth state in 1845, only 800 people lived in San Antonio. This quickly changed when people from the northeastern United States and Europe arrived in the frontier community. Many became ranchers or storekeepers.

From 1820 to 1865, the government in Texas changed hands six times: Spain, Mexico, Republic of Texas, United States, Confederacy, and back to the United States. After the Civil War, San Antonio became an important destination in the cattle drives. Ranchers brought their cattle to Military Plaza to transport them north. Later, city hall, the seat of the city government, was built in Military Plaza. By 1890, San Antonio was the largest city in Texas.

SAN ANTONIO

The Torch of Friendship (left) was a gift to San Antonio from Mexico as a sign of friendship and to represent the roots many Texans share with Mexico. The steel sculpture is 65 feet tall and weighs 50 tons. Behind it is the Tower of the Americas at HemisFair Park. Right: A monarch butterfly

Chapter

3

The San Antonio River

San Antonio is unique for more reasons than its history and culture. It is located in south-central Texas at a point where different types of landscapes meet. North of San Antonio is called Hill Country because of the many small hills with **juniper** trees. The nearby East Texas pine forests are very different from the brush country found south of the city. With its cattle ranches in the desert to the west, San Antonio was close to the many cattle routes of the nineteenth century. Because of these many geographical differences, San Antonio has always been an independent city that defies description. It's not a southern or western city; it is simply San Antonio.

With the city's varied geography and weather, visitors are likely to find plants and wildlife from the three different regions. Palm trees, cactuses, juniper trees, and all types of **deciduous** (dih-SID-joo-us) trees can be found in San Antonio's outdoors. Mistflowers bloom in the fall and attract monarch butterflies that are migrating to Mexico. One dangerous example of

Mountain lions go by many names, including puma and cougar. Native to the San Antonio area, occasional sightings are still reported. In 2007, two areas in the northwest part of town were closed after mountain lion reports.

fall color is poison ivy. Although the yellow, orange, and red leaves of autumn can be attractive, they are to be avoided. The mountain lion is native to San Antonio's Bexar County, although there are fewer now than there once were. Snakes, particularly the nonpoisonous Texas rat snake, like the warm weather found in San Antonio.

In southern Texas, winters are mild. Temperatures in San Antonio rarely drop below 41 degrees, so snowfall is rare, although rain frequently falls in the spring and early fall months. Summer brings less rain and temperatures in the mid 90s. For people driving a car, San Antonio is about the same distance from the Corpus Christi beaches at the Gulf of Mexico as it is from the Mexican border (around 150 miles).

Yet even with its unique surroundings, what has drawn people to the seventh largest city in the United States for several hundred years is the river. Starting as a trickle, the 240-mile-long San Antonio River twists and turns as it follows a path to the Gulf of Mexico.

However, the river hasn't always been kind. At times, it has carried diseases like **cholera** (KAH-luh-ruh). Some years, the river dried up and left San Antonio a drought-ridden town without much to offer. Other years, floods sent the river over its banks and into people's homes and other buildings.

A series of aqueducts started by settlers hundreds of years ago are today part of the plan that keeps the San Antonio River from flooding the city.

While fine-tuning the aqueduct network, some people with vision believed that San Antonio could be the Venice of America. The city broke ground for a two-mile-long River Walk in 1939, and soon people traveled the river on flat boats called gondolas.

La Villita was the first neighborhood in San Antonio. Located on the south bank of the river, La Villita is now a historic area that includes the Arneson River Theatre where people can watch concerts or other entertainment.

The leaders of the community decided that something needed to be done about the unpredictable river. They expanded the aqueduct system that the Spanish had started for irrigating crops in the 1700s. The early twentieth century was spent improving the aqueducts, deepening channels, and installing gates to prevent the San Antonio River from flooding city streets. What started as a public works project produced a system of brick walkways and bridges bordered by shops, theaters, and restaurants called the River Walk.

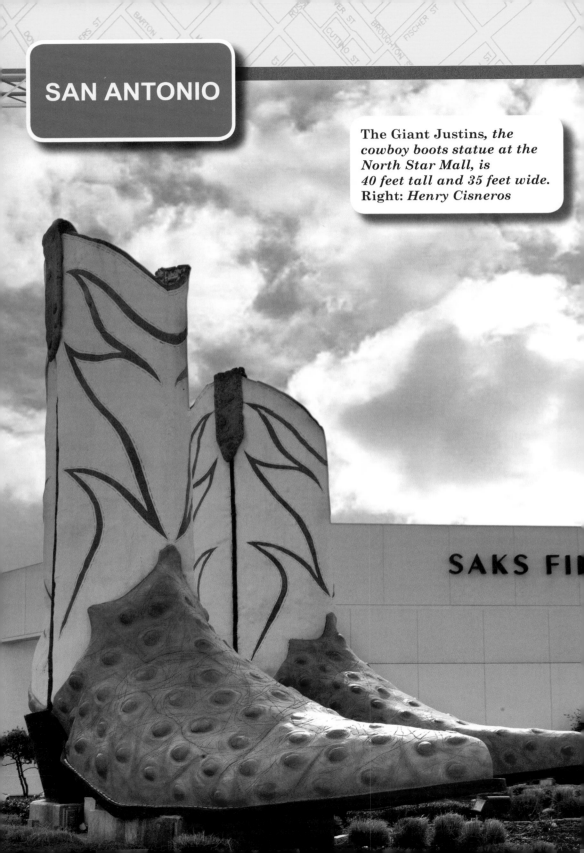

The Giant Justins, *the cowboy boots statue at the North Star Mall, is 40 feet tall and 35 feet wide.* Right: *Henry Cisneros*

SAKS FI

Chapter 4

The Many Cultures of San Antonio

Like its mixture of geography, San Antonio also has a variety of cultures. The city began with Spanish and Mexican residents, known as Tejanos. Later, Anglos— people from the United States—settled in San Antonio. After the end of the 1846–1848 war with Mexico, people arrived from England, Italy, France, Denmark, and Czechoslovakia (cheh-koh-sloh-VAH-kee-uh) to make their home in this new American city.

One of the largest groups from Europe to settle in San Antonio during the nineteenth century came from Germany. The German language was likely to be heard on San Antonio's streets, and in 1853 a German newspaper was established. The successful German ranchers and storekeepers built big Victorian homes along King William Street, south of downtown, in the last half of that century.

Today, English or Spanish are the languages most often heard in San Antonio. The majority of residents (almost 59 percent) are Hispanic. Almost 32 percent are Anglos, with a background that includes a variety of European heritages such as German.

The mesh of cultures becomes more noticeable during April, which is Fiesta time. Fiesta started as a way to celebrate Texas independence. Today, it is a ten-day festival that draws millions of people to the streets to see parades and celebrations. Lots of **mariachi** (mah-ree-AH-chee) music and different kinds of food are important parts of Fiesta too. Don't worry too much if someone breaks an egg over your head.

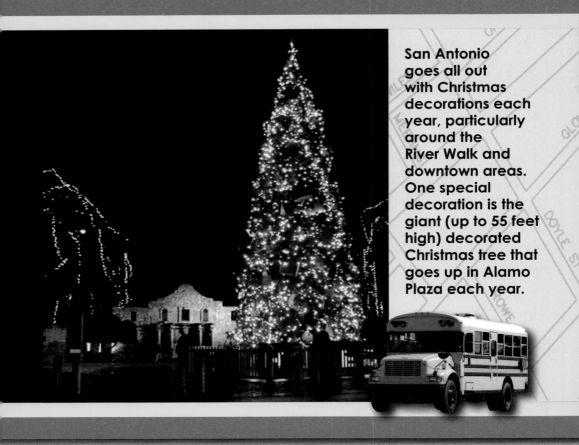

San Antonio goes all out with Christmas decorations each year, particularly around the River Walk and downtown areas. One special decoration is the giant (up to 55 feet high) decorated Christmas tree that goes up in Alamo Plaza each year.

Strolling bands of musicians called mariachis represent Mexican culture. Mariachi band members often wear charro suits and sombreros.

These are cascarones filled with colorful paper instead of eggs.

Born in San Antonio, Henry Cisneros knows about Mexican American life, because he is Mexican American. After being elected the youngest representative on the city council in 1975, Cisneros was elected the city's first Hispanic mayor in 1981. He served four terms as mayor, then became Secretary of Housing and Urban Development under President Bill Clinton.

Education has long been an important concern for San Antonio. In 1851, it became one of the first Texas cities to offer free public education for boys and girls. One graduate of San Antonio schools is comedian Carol Burnett, who began working on a children's

Another popular attraction for visitors to San Antonio is SeaWorld San Antonio. The 250-acre marine life adventure park includes shows, rides, and animal attractions.

television show in the 1950s. In the 1960s and 1970s, she had her own television show, *The Carol Burnett Show*. Her comedy sketches and funny faces made her one of America's most beloved comedians.

Residents and tourists both enjoy time at SeaWorld and the Six Flags amusement park called Fiesta Texas. Yet there's also plenty of arts and culture available in places like the McNay Art Museum, the first museum of modern art to open in Texas. The people of San

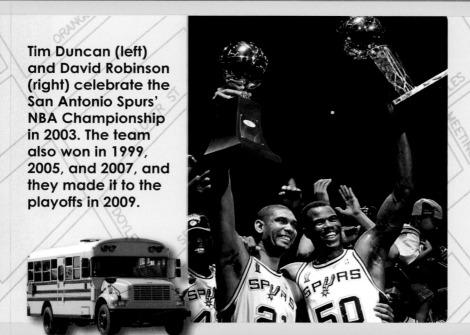

Tim Duncan (left) and David Robinson (right) celebrate the San Antonio Spurs' NBA Championship in 2003. The team also won in 1999, 2005, and 2007, and they made it to the playoffs in 2009.

Antonio are very proud of the Alamodome arena, which for nine seasons was home to the National Basketball Association team the San Antonio Spurs.

David Robinson came to San Antonio when he was drafted to play basketball for the Spurs. Nicknamed "The Admiral" because he graduated from the U.S. Naval Academy and served in the navy, Robinson won the Rookie of the Year award in his first year with the Spurs. The 7-foot, 1-inch basketball star went on to win many awards and honors during his basketball career, including two championship games. Robinson has also been important off the court in San Antonio. He gave $9 million to his adopted city to start the Carver Academy, a school for culturally diverse students.

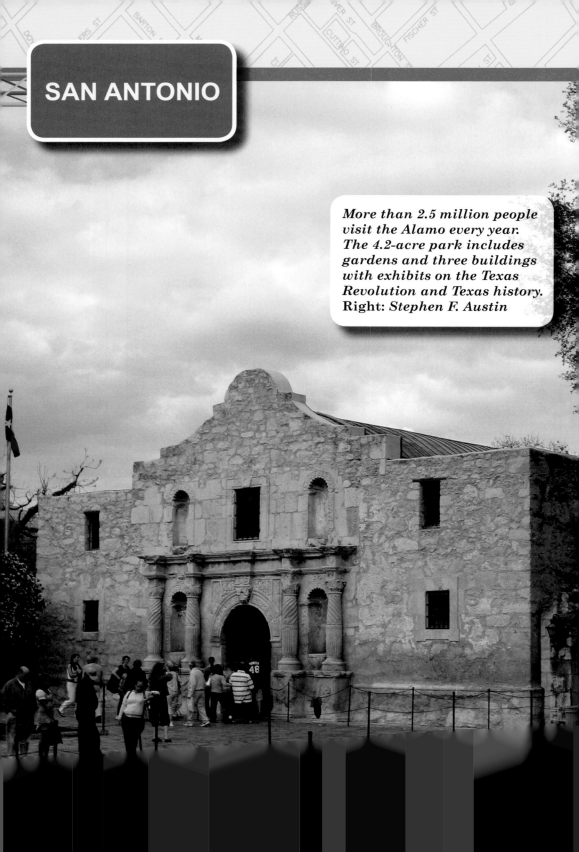

SAN ANTONIO

More than 2.5 million people visit the Alamo every year. The 4.2-acre park includes gardens and three buildings with exhibits on the Texas Revolution and Texas history. Right: Stephen F. Austin

The Class Trip to San Antonio

Maria's class boarded the school bus early the next morning. Some of her classmates fell asleep during the ride, but she was too excited to nap. She looked out the window as she felt the bus slow down, but all she saw were cars.

"Class," Ms. Hughes said, turning to face them from her seat behind the bus driver, "we're coming into San Antonio."

As the teacher reminded the students about class trip rules, Maria began looking out every window she could. She saw tall skyscrapers shining in the sun.

Her hand shot up in the air.

"Yes, Maria?"

"All I see are those modern buildings. Where is the real San Antonio?"

Ms. Hughes laughed. "Those modern buildings are the real San Antonio, Maria. San Antonio has many new buildings, but it also has old ones like the missions, La Villita, Market Square, San Fernando Cathedral—"

"Six Flags!" Tommy shouted.

31

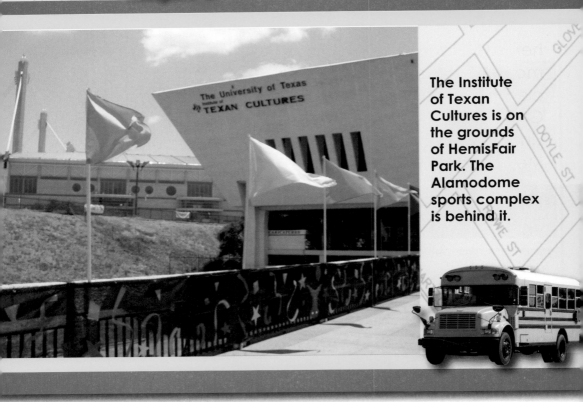

The Institute of Texan Cultures is on the grounds of HemisFair Park. The Alamodome sports complex is behind it.

Jesse added, "SeaWorld!"

The bus left the highway for the city streets. A sign showed that they were on Alamo Street, but Maria couldn't see the Alamo at all. Instead, the bus pulled into a parking lot, and the bus driver called out, "HemisFair Park." Maria's grandmother had told her that she had gone to the World's Fair in HemisFair Park in 1968.

"We've talked about the many cultures that make up San Antonio," Ms. Hughes said. "So we'll start our trip at the museum of the Institute of Texan Cultures."

As the students got off the bus, they entered a white building. After passing a large globe, they divided into groups for an hour of looking around. With her friends Maddie and Holly, Maria found exhibits for many of the cultural groups they had talked about in class, plus more that they hadn't talked about, like Greek and Chinese. There was even a Tejano exhibit. Since Maria's grandparents had come to Texas from Mexico, they were Tejanos.

The Texas Folklife Festival, held each summer, is an outdoor festival at HemisFair Park that celebrates Texas cultures. Ethnic foods, crafts, and activities; dozens of dance groups, music groups, and craft vendors; and carnival rides are just some of the festival's attractions.

The flag from the Alamo

Many exhibits had someone standing by who would talk and answer questions. Maria enjoyed the weaving demonstration near the Swedish area. They ended at the American Indian exhibit, where they heard about the Texas Folklife Festival held each summer. The outdoors festival has food, music, dancing, and other activities from more than forty different cultures. Maria decided to talk to her parents about going. It could be their summer vacation!

Instead of getting on the bus when they left the museum, the students walked across the park to reach Bowie Street. The buildings started to look older and more colorful. Many decorations lined the streets, especially around Market Street. When they crossed Market Street, they saw the San Antonio River in front of them, with cobblestone walkways and stores and restaurants on each side. Ms. Hughes said the River Walk was the most popular place for visitors to go when they visited San Antonio. Although it was a sunny day, the River Walk was shaded with palm trees.

Ms. Hughes took the class a little farther down Alamo Street to a plaza with the oldest-looking building Maria had seen so far. It was the Alamo, built in 1718. A stone wall surrounded part of it.

The class walked across the Brick Walk, engraved with the names of people who had lost their lives at the Alamo. Finally, they entered the mission. They first passed through the Long Barracks. Maria saw cases with weapons and tools that people had used during the battle. She read about the battle and the different people who had been there. She learned that the remains of the defenders were kept in a marble crypt in the San Fernando Cathedral. Although many people were touring the Alamo, everyone talked quietly, as if at a church service.

When the class left the museum, their teacher began talking to them about the San Antonio Missions National Historical Park, also called the Mission Trail. One of the unique things about San Antonio is that five missions are still standing in the city. After the Alamo, the other four make up the Mission Trail.

A weapons display at the Alamo

The class followed Ms. Hughes down some stone steps to the river. They walked along the river until they reached a boat. Ms. Hughes stood near the gangway and gestured her students on board. As smiles lit up the faces, she handed each child a paper sack. After they all took a seat, the boat started its lazy trip down the river. The students dug into their lunches and listened to the pilot talk about San Antonio.

Did You Know?

The San Antonio Missions Historical Park includes all five San Antonio missions. Operated by the National Park Service, the park also includes an original grist mill and aqueduct.

After lunch and the boat ride, Ms. Hughes reported that they would be going to another museum.

"We've already seen two today," groaned Maddie.

Maria had enjoyed the first two museums, so she didn't mind as much. It was over 80 degrees outside, and it would be cooler in the museum.

When they arrived at a light brown building, Maria had hoped it might be one of the other missions. The building looked older, but it was too tall to be a mission built by the Spanish and the Indians hundreds of years ago. A sign outside the door told them they were entering an art museum.

A young woman with a big smile came out and greeted them. "Hello, you all must be from Lincoln Elementary. I'm Ms. Gonzales. Welcome to SAMA."

"What's SAMA?" one of the students asked.

"S-A-M-A are the initials for the San Antonio Museum of Art, so we like to shorten it to SAMA. How do you like our building? We've been here since 1981, but the building is almost a hundred years older. It used to belong to the Lone Star Brewery. Today, the building holds one of the most impressive art collections in the Southwest United States. We have art from different countries in Asia, plus Greek, Roman, and Egyptian art."

Ms. Gonzales held her hand in the air. "But that's not what we're going to see today. I understand you all have been studying cultures, so we're going to find out more about one of the biggest cultural influences of San Antonio—the Hispanic influence. We'll be looking at pre-Columbian art from a really long time ago, art that was pop-ular when San Antonio was being settled, and the art of today."

For almost an hour, the class looked at paintings, drawings, and many statues. They thanked Ms. Gonzales and went outside once more.

Pre-Columbian Statue at SAMA

Maria and her friends got a chuckle from watching the polar bears play at the San Antonio Zoo. The zoo also has an aquarium, plus a bird exhibit with one of the largest collections of birds in the world.

"Class, we've visited many places today," Ms. Hughes called out. "I know you're getting tired, but we have time to see one more thing. Who here likes animals?"

As expected, the entire class waved their hands in the air, and that's how the class found their way to the San Antonio Zoo. Although they didn't have time to visit all of the zoo's 3,500 animals, they did get to see the hundreds of butterflies at the Caterpillar Flight School, baby condors, and many other unusual animals. It was the perfect end to a perfect day for Maria and her classmates.

Just The Facts

Founded: 1718; city incorporated 1837

Location: South-central Texas, approximately 140 miles northwest of the Gulf of Mexico and 150 miles northeast of the city of Laredo on the Mexican border. San Antonio is the seat of Bexar (pronounced "bear") County.

Form of Government: Mayor

Land Area: 408 square miles

Population in 2008: 1.32 million

Percent of Population Under 18: 28.5%

U.S. Rank: The 7th most populous city in the U.S.

Density: Approximately 3200 people per square mile

Latitude: 29° 32'N

Longitude: 98° 28'W

Average Elevation: 701 feet above sea level

Highest Point: Tower of the Americas at 750 feet

Average High: 80°F

Average Low: 58°F

Hottest Month: July

Coldest Month: January

Average Annual Precipitation: 33 inches

Major Industries: Tourism, agriculture (crops, cattle, sheep), manufacturing, military (5 military installations), medical, telecommunications, biotechnology

Major Neighborhoods: Castle Hills, Dignowity Hill, King William Historical District, La Villita, Pecan Valley

Public Parks: Brackenridge Park, Braunig Lake Park, Calaveras Lake Park, Casa Navarro State Historical Park, Eisenhower Park, HemisFair Park, McAllister Park, San Antonio Botanical Gardens

Major Sports Teams: Missions—Minor League Baseball; Spurs—Basketball; Silver Stars—Women's Basketball; Rampage—Minor League Hockey

Major Museums and Cultural Centers: The Institute of Texan Cultures, San Antonio Museum of Art, San Antonio Missions National Historical Park, McNay Art Museum, El Mercado (Market Square)

Cascarones

A cascaron is a colorful eggshell filled with confetti. When it is broken over someone's head, it means good fortune will rain down upon that person. Cascarones were originally made in Mexico, where they are often used at Easter. In San Antonio, cascarones are popular at Fiesta time.

What You Need:

raw eggs
thumbtack
butter knife
bowl of warm soapy water
towel
confetti*

colored tissue paper
scissors
white glue
decorations such as egg dye, markers, tempera paint, or glitter

* You can buy packaged confetti or you can make your own. Cut up paper into very small pieces. You can use old newspapers, magazines, and even junk mail. If you know someone with a three-hole paper punch, you can also empty it for confetti.

What You Do:

1. Decide what type of decoration you will use. If you're going to use egg dye, then dye the eggs before you do the following steps. If you're using markers or paint, empty the eggs first.

2. Poke a hole on top of the egg with a thumbtack.

3. Gently tap the other end of the egg with a butter knife until you have a dime-sized hole. Break the yolk with the thumbtack, then empty the yolk and white from the egg.

4. Rinse the eggs, then wash them with warm soapy water. Allow them to dry completely. Be gentle; remember that eggshells are fragile. Wash your hands well after cleaning the eggs.

5. If you didn't dye your eggs before emptying them, decorate them now with markers or paint. Make them colorful!

6. Use a spoon to add confetti through the holes in the cascarones.

7. Glue a small piece of colored tissue paper over the hole. Allow the glue to dry before handling the cascarones.

When you are ready to celebrate, you don't want to conk anyone on the head with the cascaron. Instead, break it open and let the confetti shower down on the person.

San Antonio Historical Timeline

1709   San Antonio River is named by Espinosa-Olivares-Aguirre expeditions.

1718   Mission San Antonio de Valero is established on the west bank of the San Antonio River. It will be moved two times, in 1719 and in 1724, to its final location. In May, the fort San Antonio de Béxar Presidio is founded.

1720   Mission San José y San Miguel de Aguayo is established.

1722   Presidio is moved to Military Plaza.

1731   Spanish colonists from the Canary Islands arrive, and a town council is established. Three East Texas missions are moved to San Antonio: Mission Concepción, Mission San Juan, and Mission San Francisco de la Espada.

1738   Construction on San Fernando Church is started.

1749   "Governor's Palace" is built in San Antonio.

1756   The present Alamo chapel is built as Mission San Antonio de Valero.

1772   San Antonio becomes the seat of government for New Spain.

1789   First non-mission school is opened in San Antonio.

1821   Mexico wins independence from Spain.

1822   Banco Nacional de Texas is organized. It is the first national bank west of the Mississippi.

1836   Texas declares independence from Mexico. Texas loses the battle of the Alamo to General Santa Anna, who is later defeated in the Battle of San Jacinto. Bexar County is organized.

1837   First city council meeting is held. Texas Legislature approves incorporating the "City of San Antonio."

1841   First modern bridge across the San Antonio River is built at Commerce Street from cypress and cedar logs.

1845   Texas becomes the twenty-eighth state.

1846   First U.S. Post Office is established in San Antonio.

1848   San Antonio's first newspaper, *The Western Texan*, is published.

San Antonio Historical Timeline

1851   First public schools open in San Antonio.

1876   Construction begins at Fort Sam Houston.

1877   First passenger train reaches San Antonio.

1890   City Hall is built.

1905   Daughters of the Republic of Texas take over care of the Alamo, preventing its destruction.

1913   San Antonio's Spanish-language newspaper *La Prensa* begins publication.

1921   The worst flood in San Antonio history damages downtown.

1939   River Walk improvement project begins.

1941   San José Mission is named a National Historical Site.

1950   The state's first modern art museum, Marion Koogler McNay Art Institute, is established.

1968   The World's Fair, called HemisFair '68, opens. The Institute of Texan Cultures opens; it will become part of the University of Texas in 1973.

1973   National Basketball Association team the San Antonio Spurs begins its first season.

1988   SeaWorld of Texas opens.

1992   Fiesta Texas opens and becomes a yearly event.

1999   The San Antonio Spurs win their first NBA Championship.

2003   The San Antonio Spurs win their second NBA Championship.

2005   The San Antonio Spurs win their third NBA Championship.

2007   The San Antonio Spurs win their fourth NBA Championship.

2008   The City of San Antonio begins a $345 million improvement project to extend the length of the River Walk from three to thirteen miles.

2009   Museum Reach—in which the River Walk will be connected to four missions and other museums—is scheduled to be completed.

Further Reading

Books

Kimmel, Eric A. *The Lady in the Blue Cloak: Legends from the Texas Missions*. New York: Holiday House, 2006.

Levy, Janey. *The Alamo: A Primary Source History of the Legendary Texas Mission (Primary Sources in American History)*. New York: Rosen Publishing Group, 2002.

Murphy, Jim. *Inside the Alamo*. New York: Delacorte, 2003.

Stout, Mary. *San Antonio (Great Cities of the World)*. Strongsville, OH: World Almanac Library, 2005.

Warrick, Karen Clemens. *Alamo: Victory of Death on the Texas Frontier (America's Living History)*. Berkeley Heights, NJ: Enslow Publishers, 2008.

Internet Sources

The Alamo
    http://www.thealamo.org

The City of San Antonio
    http://www.uthscsa.edu/micro/city.html

San Antonio Convention & Visitors Bureau
    http://www.visitsanantonio.com

San Antonio Missions National Historical Park
    http://www.nps.gov/saan

San Antonio Natural Areas
    http://www.sanaturalareas.org

San Antonio Riverwalk
    http://www.sanantonioriverwalk.com

Works Consulted

Fisher, Lewis F. *Crown Jewel of Texas*. San Antonio: Maverick Publishing Co., 1997.

———. *San Antonio: Outpost of Empires*. San Antonio: Maverick Publishing Co., 1997.

Hawrocki, Susanna, and Gerald Lair. *San Antonio: Portrait of a Fiesta City*. Stillwater, MN: Voyageur Press, 1992.

Ketcherside, Erik. *City Smart Guidebook: San Antonio (2nd edition)*. Santa Fe, NM: John Muir Publications, 1999.

Moore, Rolf E. *"The Texas Coahuiltecan Indians."* http://www.texasindians.com/

Permenter, Paris, and John Bigley. *Insiders' Guide to San Antonio (Third Edition)*. Guilford, CT: Globe Pequot Press, 2006.

Texas State Historical Association. *Handbook of Texas Online*. http://www.tshaonline.org/

Todish, Tim J., and Terry S. Todish. *Alamo Sourcebook 1836*. Austin: Eakin Press, 1998.

Glossary

aqueduct (AK-wuh-dukt)—A large channel built to carry water across land.

cholera (KAH-luh-ruh)—A serious disease that causes severe diarrhea.

deciduous (dih-SID-joo-us) **trees**—Trees that shed their leaves every year.

drought (DROUT)—A long period of dry weather without rain or snow.

grist (GRIST) **mill**—A place to grind grain.

Hispanic (his-PAN-ik)—A person who lives in the United States but whose ancestors come from Spanish speaking America.

juniper (JOO-nih-pur)—An evergreen bush or short tree that looks like a pine.

mariachi (mah-ree-AH-chee)—A type of music that originated in Mexico and features singing, trumpets, guitars, and violins.

mission (MIH-shun)—A place created by missionaries to do religious or charitable works.

nomadic (noh-MAD-ik)—Wandering from place to place to follow food or good weather.

plaza (PLAH-zuh)—An open area, usually a public square.

presidio (preh-SEE-dee-oh)—A military post originally under Spanish control.

siege (SEEJ)—A military tactic to surround a place and cut off supplies and food until surrender.

Texian (TEK-see-un)—A non-native person who lived in Texas before it became a state.

Index

ABOUT THE AUTHOR

Karen Bush Gibson writes about people, places, and events for the school library market. Her books for Mitchell Lane Publishers include *Mudslide in La Conchita, CA, 2005; The Vietnam War;* and *The Historic Fight for the 2008 Democratic Nomination: The Obama View.* Gibson lives in Oklahoma, a neighbor to Texas. San Antonio is one of her favorite cities, and one that she visits as often as she can.